Honk

～

Honk

Poems by

Tony Gruenewald

Cover design by Shay Culligan

ISBN: 978-1-63980-048-3

Kelsay Books
502 South 1040 East, A-119
American Fork, Utah 84003
Kelsaybooks.com

For Amanda for finally making it easy.
For John and Gina Larkin for the friendship, love, and support.

Acknowledgments

Big Hammer: "Red, White, Black, and Blue"

Duck Lake Journal: "The Revolution Will Be Monetized"

Edison Literary Review: "Where I'm From (after George Ella Lyon);" "Sequel;" "Assimilation;" "Einstein's Geese;" "America Achieved Along the New Jersey Turnpike;" "Junior High School"

Exit 13: "Off Duty;" "After the Midnight Ride of Tony Smith;" "Appalachian League Friday Night;" "King George Road;" "Mile Marker 116;" "Echocardiogram Blues;" "To the Candidates of the Masters of Fine Arts Program"

Lummox: "The Later Middle Ages;" "Substitute"

Mas Tequila Review: "Joy to the World;" "Statistically Insignificant"

Santa Clara Review: "Punctuation"

Spitball: "Baseball Ekphrasis: 1965 Roger Maris Topps #155;" "Baseball Ekphrasis: 1965 Casey Stengel Topps #187"

Ragazine: "Names Were Changed to Protect... (or, The Things My Grandfathers Did to Survive);" "The Optometrics of Love"

Tiferet: "Down to Earth;" "A Day in the Life"

U.S. 1 Worksheets: "Guernica;" "The Desecration of the Secret Chihuahua Burial Ground;" "Pulaski Skyway"

U.S. 1 Newspaper: "Escalate;" "Which Way is Up?;" "Avoiding the Obvious on The New Jersey Turnpike"

Your Daily Poem: "Joy to the World;" "Einstein's Geese;" "America Achieved Along the New Jersey Turnpike;" "Down to Earth;" "A Day in the Life"

Contents

Avoiding the Obvious on The New Jersey Turnpike

Because of the overnight construction,
five lanes of traffic were being threaded
through the eye of a single lane.

And from behind the lights
of the radio mentioning
every delay but the one I was in,

all I could see was
an assuredly God-sent sign,
a panoramic view of

a pig's behind,
painted across the back
of the tractor-trailer

directly ahead of me,
leaving me with slowly moving
miles and miles of nothing to do

but to try to ignore
the Lord's metaphor
for how I've been living my life.

Which Way Is Up?

The sports car slingshots past me,
the morning sun sparkling
off its shining silver skin,
its license plate singing
"Upbeat"
as it effortlessly slides
through the Monday morning
commute, increasing
the distance
between us.

It's been years since
I've had a car
that stated anything,
or even asked for attention,
my weather-worn Hyundai
after a decade
still as efficient and anonymous
as the workers who assembled it.
Road weary,
taken for granted,
too humbled
to demand tags
that grumble
a bashful
"Beat Up"
to the heedless world
brashly passing by.

Assimilation

As with most immigrant groups,
after several generations
they're totally acculturated
to their surroundings,
in this case
an artificial island
filling the middle
of a swamp
disguised as
a Princeton office park.

On the way to our cars
my colleague notes that
they're no longer
polite enough
to be Canadian Geese,

their assimilated honking
no longer distinguishable
from the irritated sounds
emanating from the gaggle
of commuters
we're about to join
on our congested
migratory path
commonly known as
the Route 1 corridor.

Pulaski Skyway

A permanent exhibition
caught mid-stride
crossing its imagined
swampy domain
a dinosaur
guessed together
by puzzled paleontologists
in this Museum of Unnatural History

Cars skitter along its skeleton
like parasites desperate to pick
the last morsel of asphalt
from its steely spine

Einstein's Geese

Some Princetonians believe
that simply living within
the 08540 postal zone
adds at least
20 points to an IQ.

And they must be convinced
that even the resident geese
that loiter at the office parks
and on the outskirts of town
are literate.

How else can one explain
the sign?

The sign that had to cost enough
to feed and clothe
a family of four for months
in an underdeveloped country.

The sign that reads, "NO GEESE,"
and for added emphasis adds
a picture of a goose
inside the universal
red slashed circle.

And being Princeton geese,
they ignore the sign anyway,
having also inherited
that ivied sense
of entitlement.

While in my neighborhood,
the geese lean on
the black plywood hunting dog silhouettes
meant to discourage them,
smoking cigarettes and making
goose calls at passing women.

And even the park police are
intimidated. When you call to complain,
they confide in hushed tones,
"There's nothing we can do...
It's best to try to ignore them."

Appalachian League Friday Night

Beyond the outfield fences
where every spot in the lot
has a "Park at Your Own Risk" warning,
twilight highlights the towering beacons
of McDonald's, Wendy's, and Cracker Barrel signs
that beckon travelers off the interstate
to the town's main drag.

On our way to the park
we take a chance on
a strip mall sushi joint
full of folks
in camouflage, work shirts, and tank tops
eating teriyaki out of styrofoam
and it turns out
the sushi is surprisingly good.

I try to tamp down my Jersey
and tune my ears to West Virginia
as the ticket taker tells us
we can sit anywhere except
where the season ticket-holders' names
are laminated to
the backs of their seats.

While inside we're outsiders:
Surrounded by season ticketholders,
it feels like we've intruded on
a nightly family reunion.

During warmups the opposing team's players laugh
as the local smile-in-his-voice baritone
blunders his way through

their Latino names
while announcing the lineups.
The home team's long lanky teenaged lefty
looks the part
with his effortless delivery and blond locks
flowing from beneath his flat-billed cap,
but he's learning that
even Rookie League hitters
can turn on his easy heat,
putting a few windshields
beyond the right field fence
in peril whenever
he leaves it down the middle.

Since the park shares
property with a school,
there's no beer here,
so the sober heckling sounds
slightly more family-friendly
than, say, Philadelphia.

After the game I wonder aloud,
"We know how the guys
from the Dominican and Venezuela
got here, but how did the chefs
bring their sushi
to the strip mall
nestled between
a Dollar General and
Dove's Custom Guns?"

After the Midnight Ride of Tony Smith

...[The New Jersey Turnpike] did something for me that art had never done.
—Sculptor Tony Smith

Brutalism is an architectural style of the 1950s and 1960s characterized by simple, block-like forms and raw concrete construction.
—Tate Galleries website

Before *Time* titled him
Master of Monumentalism,
Tony Smith took his clandestine
Midnight Ride on the far-from-finished
New Jersey Turnpike.

As he witnessed what he called
"The end of art,"
did his headlights, like mine,
illumine a litany
of towering Hindu deities
straddling the swamp

whose many skeletal arms
support the high-tension wires;
that power the Budweiser eagle
as it hovers in its endless holding pattern
just beyond Newark Airport?

As he passed,
did the moonlight shimmer on
the statues sculpted of
scrapyard steel and aluminum?

Did he know this installation
would become the country's
most notorious monument
to Brutalism? Brutalism,

its real meaning
and its misnomer,
in this case, are
both true:
Since the Turnpike is
that 144 mile masterpiece
of unadorned concrete, asphalt, and steel
whose function obliterated form

And now, as in most museums,
you pay for the privilege
to visit these most victorious invasive species
as they slash through
the swamp and farmland
of this Garden State gone by
whose Secretary of Agriculture
once warned,
"Asphalt is the last crop."

Ode to Sandhogs
(after Billy Collins "Subway")

Sandhog—a laborer who works in underwater or underground excavation and construction (such as in the building of tunnels or bridge foundations)
—Merriam-Webster

And the children of Israel shall go on dry ground through the midst of the sea.
—Exodus 14:16 NKJV

When Moses parted the Red Sea there was a couple of Sandhogs there.
—A Sandhog legend

I wish I had the faith in the Lord
that I bestow upon these tunnels
that part the Hudson River
for my pleasure
and through which I travel
in the bellies
of silver-skinned Leviathans,
created just to sport in them.

I wish my faith in the Lord
would match that of
the holy Sandhogs
who dared to dig and dynamite,
blast and burrow these tunnels
through the bedrock and muck
with a hundred feet
of riverbed and water
propped precariously
above their heads
so we all could go on dry ground
in the midst of the sea.

I slide through these tunnels
like a poor person
through the eye of a needle
because those holy Sandhogs
prayed to defy death
while they descended daily
into an airless abyss
and revealed more than
the mustard seed of faith
I can barely muster.

America is blessed
by its meek
for they shall inherit
the job everybody else
believes is beneath them
or isn't desperate enough
to be driven underground
by the hunger to feed a family
in a world that tried to roll up
its welcome mat whenever
it saw them limp
toward its door
to do.

So, every time you glide assuredly
along these steely rails
and paths of asphalt
please say a prayer in praise
of the holy Sandhogs
who gave their lives

to make these rocks
of ages cleft for you
so that you might gain
the luxury to complain
as loudly as
an Israelite fleeing Egypt

that your bus or train
is late

again.

Native Species

We once paid a visit to San Diego
where the ocean and desert meet,
creating a climatic conflict that produces
plant life that looks like
it's been plucked from the pages
of a story by Dr. Seuss.

We later learn
it's Seuss's adopted hometown
and it's obvious the Truffula trees
that populate the landscapes of his stories
were not the fantasy flora
of a fervid imagination, but
the familiar Monterey Cypress
he saw outside his window.

In whose limbs, perhaps, he observed
the native zinn-a-zu bird perched
safely out of reach
of an indigenous
star-bellied sneetch
that he watched while stroking
his own mischievous
top-hatted cat.

Down to Earth

The gnarled, who-knows-how-old oak
leans alarmingly to the east
much to the consternation of, I'm sure,
the owner of the property
next to the cemetery.

For centuries its roots have fed
from the Revolutionary era remains
buried beneath it. We know because
it's been swallowing, decade-by-decade,
the headstones beside it,
parts of which now
protrude from its trunk
like mummified elephant ears.

Just as the centuries have erased
the names of the interred
from the stones' engravings
I fear for that day
the historical society summons
the arborist who will gravely stare
and suggest its reduction to sawdust
even as squirrels still scamper
amongst its now brittle branches.

And upon my demise
do not make my marker
of sandstone or marble,
but of wood and bark
nourished by my remains
to create another

sanctuary for the sparrows
and skyscraper for the squirrels,
and whose leaves, when full,
offer shelter from the sun
and after they've fallen,
return me unto dust
again.

Mile Marker 116

A car pulls off to the shoulder
of the Jersey Turnpike where
the snow has been grudgingly ground
down to an icy mound of soot.

A dejected-looking family sits inside,
but since I'm streaking by
at seventy-something,
it's too fast to stop,
so I say a quick prayer
that roadside assistance is
both swift and
inexpensive.

But for a second I think,
"This is Jersey, ya know,"
and after seeing the Pulaski Skyway
hanging like the black bunting of a memorial
on the grimy grey horizon

I know this could be where
they observe their vigil,
mile marker 116 being as close
to a gravestone as they have,
where his family suspects
the Family sent Uncle Jimmy
to his eternal rest,

below the amber waves
of winter cattails
that feed off of this and
the answers to other mysteries
forever buried
in the muck
of the Meadowlands.

Joy to the World

Dear Mr. Bus Driver,
I am so sorry it has taken more than forty years
to apologize on behalf of the 60-something
sixth graders, teachers and chaperones
who surely shaved years off your life
while you drove us to and from someplace
I've long ago forgotten
for a field trip memorable only
for the following moments
shared on your bus
in the spring of '71.

We had transistor radios enough
to fill your bus with the sounds
of WABC, the biggest, brashest
Top Forty station
in the biggest, brashest city
in the nation
which would play its number one song,
at least once every half hour,
sometimes more if the song was huge,
which this one was—
in the midst of
seven whopping weeks atop
the almighty
Music Power survey,
sandwiched between
another two weeks
at number two!

So, every twenty-some minutes
between Ike and Tina, the Temptations,
and the Partridge Family
those organ chords,
wrenched the attention
of every sixth grader, teacher, and chaperone
from whatever we were doing
to on cue
scream:

JEREMIAH WAS A BULLFROG

How this did not drive you
to drive us
off the road
or into some other
unsuspecting vehicle
was, in retrospect,
to witness
a miracle
and is an act
worthy of
at least a bullet point
on the résumé of
someone deserving
sainthood.

The Revolution will be Monetized

On a grainy day
in a diner in the camo-clad
soul of Pennsylvania
I'm eating an omelet
under the gaze of pretty boy Elvis,

who's behind the counter
serving Bogie, Monroe, and Dean,
that core four who
laid their lives to waste by haste
and living masters' classes of bad habits.

They're forever frozen
above our booth in
the always-present poster of
"Boulevard of Broken Dreams."

Heinwein's Hopper parody's lonely
lessons were long ago lost
to the tentacles of nostalgia,
leaving it as flaccid as the camouflage
worn by almost every other guy in the place.

The only hunting anyone here today will do
is for Christmas gifts for the grandchildren
whose ironed-on images
smile out from the sweatshirts of the women
who stream to and from the restroom

as a half-century-ago
Mick Jagger leers, "I can't get no…"

on the golden oldies station's
playlist of predigested songs
cashed out of their souls.
The anarchic sting of "Satisfaction"
now neutralized by its familiarity,
renders Keith Richard's rude riffs
more comforting than
the meatloaf on the menu.

A Day in the Life

I did not see them on *The Ed Sullivan Show*.
I did not watch them perform "She Loves You" or "All My
    Loving."
The family was not gathered around the tv,
but was gathering at my grandparents' house
where my grandmother had just quietly died
while napping next to me on the couch.

I don't know if we'd have been watching that night,
but all afternoon her radio had been abuzz
with news of the arrival of
something called "the Beatles."

So, with no older siblings to school me,
I asked, "Grandma, what are the Beatles?"
My last and lasting memory of her is
her answer: "They're just boys
the girls all like—
so they throw candy at them,"
her explanation using
the currency of confection
an expression of affection she knew
my four-year-old mind could comprehend.

Junior High School

Lost in the limbo
between being cute as buttons
and almost-adulthood,
we were separated,
for society's sake

Sequestered to a citadel
where schoolyard bullies
perfected new tortures
undetected by teachers
who wondered why
we weren't learning
while distracted
by the survival-of-the-cruelest
credo of gym class
and the terror of
the treacherous trip
to the smoke-soaked
boys room.

Decades later,
I drive by my fortress of torment
and wonder where
the guard towers
and barred windows
of my barbed wire-spiked memory
have gone.

Sequel

The record-breaking temperatures melted deep layers of permafrost. And reindeer carcasses—infected with the deadly bacteria—rose to the surface of the thawing mud.

—Michaeleen Doucleff, NPR News

Does no one remember
The Blob,
that gelatinous mass
blessed with locomotion
well on its way
to consuming
the population
of Pennsylvania
until Steve McQueen and his band
of Brylcreemed clichés
saved civilization?

How soon we forget
how the feds dropped it,
freeze dried to submission,
into the Arctic ice
to, in theory, sleep it off
for eternity.

But now, in spite of alarms of
punctured ozone, melting ice caps,
and climate change,
we have forgotten
there's a giant glob
of homicidal Jello
slowly awakening from
its 60-year slumber.

So, I scan society
looking for a modern misunderstood subset
that can suck up the savvy
to save us

Because Steve McQueen,
with his icy blue cool, is long gone,
and there's no one left in Hollywood
that's hip enough
to rescue us
again.

Escalate

At work we used to report problems,
but now we're asked to escalate them
to the person tasked with their repair.
During my childhood I learned the word
from the *Evening News* and,
according to Walter Cronkite,
escalate always meant
more napalm, bombs,
and caskets coming home,

all of which seem a bit extreme
for the fixing of a link
on our company website.

Names Were Changed to Protect...
or,
(The Things My Grandfathers Did to Survive)

1. John

They all called him Johnny K, anyway.
All but the many who heard

Kanciewicz

and told him to get out,
stay out and never come back.

So, he cleaved a couple of syllables
for the sake of a job

Any job

railroad bull or driving a suicide load
across the mountains to keep himself

and his orphaned brothers and sisters
and later his two daughters and wife

and then me

alive.

2. Lutz

If he hadn't been Herr Doktor,
would he have had the nerve
to insist on a fair exchange
of a vowel for the umlaut

the Ellis Island clerk
was going to take anyway
when the alternative was spelled
Dachau?

The Substitute

The son of my father
as the Son of God
again
and he's about to be
crucified
for the second time
this Palm Sunday

as I act as
my congregation's
stand-in Paschal Lamb,

sacrificed to save
this fallen humanity
of which I'm
a most sinful
member-in-full.

While we re-
enact the Passion
I hear

the stand-in Judas,
Peter, Pilate, and
once-hosannahing mob

betray, deny, and
condemn me,

like the Nazis
and a complicit
Christian Europe

betrayed, denied
and condemned
my father's family.

And though
this not-quite-Semite
is just a substitute

King of the Jews,
I feel I've failed
my flock;

as I'm struck again
they scatter,
millennia after millennia,
fallen over and over
over and over…

Baseball Ekphrasis: 1965 Yogi Berra Topps #470

Obviously, an older picture,
the navy pinstripes peeking
from beneath his chest protector
belie the Mets flag
flapping next to his name.

I unwrapped this card
when I was five;
when I thought nothing
of cheering for both
the Yankees and the Mets.
It would be years before
I was told I had to choose:
Love one—
despise the other.

Either way, Yogi,
of course,
is smiling.

Baseball Ekphrasis: 1965 Casey Stengel Topps #187

All the photos
for these cards
are posed or portraits
except, perhaps, this one:
Casey's reclined on
the cracked dugout steps
faced away from the field,
bat retired against a leg,
with both hands and mouth
captured in mid-Stengelese story,
maybe about how
the only mistake he made
when he managed the Yankees
was the sin of turning 70.
This, for baseball's
grizzled griot at 73,
is his action shot.

Baseball Ekphrasis: 1965 Roger Maris Topps #155

North Dakota born,
he was made
for Yankee Stadium,
but not New York.
This Depression baby's
now joyless gaze
as resigned as
Dorothea Lange's
"Migrant Mother."

Red, White, Black, and Blue

The final pro football team
to integrate was
Washington.
The Redskins
acquired Bobby Mitchell
for the 1962 season.

Like in the movies
these Redskins
were not indigenous,
they had always been
pale skinned.

To celebrate,
his new owner,
George Preston Marshall
presented Mitchell
at a pre-season banquet
for players, ticket holders,
and the Washington press corps
and demanded his new star
lead his team
in a chorus
of "Dixie."

Echocardiogram Blues

Black people lived right by the railroad tracks, and the train would shake
their houses at night. I would hear it as a boy, and I thought: I'm gonna
make a song that sounds like that.
                                                    —Little Richard Penniman

You cannot live without rhythm. Does everybody agree with that? People
who don't agree with that are dead.
                                                    —Amiri Baraka

Get rhythm when you get the blues
                —Johnny Cash

Lying on my side on the examining table,
we're listening to the blood's whoosh and swoosh
as it slowly pulses
through the metronome of my heart,
when outside the window
the wheels of the express to Washington
rattle their rhythm along the rails
and my heart wants to be riding
Little Richard's locomotive of a piano
from Lucille clear through
to Bama Lama Bama Loo,
but, like Johnny Cash,
it's still stuck in this Folsom Prison
and time
            keeps
                        draggin'
                                    on.

Untitled

(September 11, 2001) photograph by Jeff Mermelstein

Ash laden leaves
on late summer trees
defy the medium.
Only obscured red lights
of a distant ambulance
confirm Fujicolor.

In the foreground a
statue, a man sitting,
seeming so obsessed
by a book
he's oblivious to the
220 stories brought
down 'round his knees.

At the Jewish Museum exhibition,
almost a year to the day,
a toddler studies this scene
from his mother's arms
and asks,

Why the city broken?

Punctuation

(for Trayvon Martin)

The bullet
put a period
where a comma
should have preceded
the promise
of and.

The Later Middle Ages

This is the Age of Knowing…
—Tagline from a pharmaceutical ad

This is the age of knowing
that when I walk
through the waiting room
the cable news channel
will be airing
a commercial
from some law firm
fishing for clients
that claim harm
from the med that's
meant to ensure me
against an eternity of
waltzing down hospital halls
in a backless gown with
an IV pole partner.

This is the age of knowing
that despite its litany
of risks
when the concerned
pharmacist asks,
"You know this prescription costs…"
an amount that could induce
a medical emergency in itself
I have no option
but to shrug and say,
"It beats the alternative."

This is the age of knowing
the music I grew up with
has grown too old

for even the oldies station
programmed to numb
the medically-induced anxiety
of the pharmacy's
targeted demographic.
This is the age of knowing
the pretty faces on
the cover of the gossip rag
at the checkout
declared to be
the sexiest people alive are
not only totally
foreign to me
but appear to be
younger than my children.

And this is the age of knowing
that the next time
anyone will market to me again
is when it
finally has
my Medicare dollars
to squander.

Guernica

It was homegrown terror
undetected until
second grade when
the nurse sent the note home
and optometrists prescribed
a lifetime of lenses
growing incrementally thicker
and more complex
masking interior Impressionism
until middle age
announced itself
with a personal meteor shower
inciting the body to attack back,
provoking a counter-insurgency
twisting the left eye's response
into visions of Guernica—

Its Surrealism at war with
the right's artificially refracted
artifice of Realism—

Two eyes so stylistically opposed—
one sees Picasso
the other an Andrew Wyeth
each fighting for primacy in
the Gallery of my Occipital Lobe.

King George Road

Not far from Washington Rock,
the Watchung Mountain overlook
where the future father of our country
observed enemy troop movements,
runs King George Road
still named for the intolerable tyrant
whose oppression sparked
the American Revolution.

The conspiracy theorist in me wonders:
is the name retained as a grim reminder or
is it a Redcoat refuge,
a secret society of Royalists conspiring
to reclaim the colonies for the crown?

Just as I'm wary that
flowing a mere cannonball's shot
from the Pentagon is a six-lane named
Jefferson Davis Highway.

Statistically Insignificant

(A thought on Steven Pinker's The Better Angels of Our Nature.)

Celebrating our evolved civility,
the author wields detailed diagrams
that present the percentage
of the American population
killed in wars in 2005 to be
what he calls,
"paint thin and
invisible."

And I know a number
cruncher who will
matter-of-factly
tell you that
when you divide
945 dead by almost
300 million living
the result is
"statistically
insignificant."

Except

when
one
of the insignificant
is 100 percent of your son or daughter
or husband or wife
or brother or sister
or mother or father
or anyone you love
and that equals

everything.

The Optometrics of Love

Thank you for being the one
who never looked
through lenses distorted
by the residue
of former boyfriends,
spouses, and lovers
and saw
me.

The Desecration of the Sacred Chihuahua Burial Ground

Two temporary mountain ranges have been driven up
from an equally ephemeral valley
in the lot across the street.

Yet, animal activists have not protested
what we old-timers know is
the desecration of a sacred chihuahua burial ground.

The owner three owners ago
bred some strange strain of
assault chihuahua there;

a miniature militia
tormenting neighbors and passersby,
including the occasional stray Shepherd

who, whimpering, would need
to be rescued after an attack
so savagely conceived and carried out

it could be chronicled as a canon of military strategy.
Years later their little willing warrior bones were buried
where a new basement will soon be sunk

to sprout at least two new stories
where ethereal banshee yips
will growl up from the basement and

through the walls to wake
the eventual owners who will find
their ankles bleeding,

riddled by the marks
of a million
tiny teeth.

To the Candidates of the Master of Fine Arts Program...

Dear Poets,
We, the Gods of Ancient Greece ask you,
no, beg you,
no, implore you
to resist the urge
to drop our names
in the poems you will feel
pressured to write to impress
your peers and instructors.

We all already know our deeds
all too well,
because your predecessors
have refused to let them rest,
rehashing our foibles
in libraries of books of poems
that are plagiarized
from the scandal sheets
of Ancient Greece.

And we think the types of poems
you wrote before you matriculated,
the tales of the kids
you shot hoops with
in the shadows
of the empty factories
of your crumbled rustbelt town,
or your fellow carpet layers
and conduit runners,
builders of the office parks

of the Great Northwest,
are much more interesting
than anything you can add
to our legends.

So please don't fall
for the inevitable temptation
to drag our ink-stained names
across yet another sheet of paper,
even if you're compelled to write
about your cousin, the one who drives
your family crazy by hogging the bathroom
to admire his flawless face
in the mirror,
while at the playground you notice
your son on the swing set
soaring perilously close
to the sun.

Off Duty

My brother-in-law, the paramedic,
stopped counting the rescues,
or worse, the recoveries
he's made on the rocks
or along the rapids
of the waterfalls
here in DuPont State Forest.

On his day off
We walk along a trail
And stop to watch
As a family slides past the sign
That shouts:
DO NOT CLIMB ON THE ROCKS.

Our families go on ahead
and while we talk, he watches
hand on the holster
of his every ready
walkie-talkie
until satisfied
there will be
no emergency
this time.

As we turn to catch up
to our kin
he gives one last look
at the family
now beyond the falls
and says,
they're what we call
job security.

America Achieved Along the New Jersey Turnpike

Although all are not
created equal,
America's most
egalitarian institution is
the rest area,

where only the display
of a handicapped
parking tag offers
any semblance of
advantage.

And while we assess the merits
of the facility
on criteria of cleanliness, perception of
safety, refreshment selection,
and hand-drying technology,

everyone—the biker, the banker,
the trooper, the trucker,
the lawyer, the laborer
the chauffeur and the chauffeured—
every ripple in the roiling river of humanity

called America
has to scramble past
the temptations of fast food
and vending machines
to tend to the business

no one, no matter how rich
or otherwise powerful, can outsource,
ignore, or pay someone
under the table to
attend to.

Where I'm From

(after George Ella Lyon)

I am from mortgage payments
wagered on parlays
and daily doubles.

I am from the rotary phone,
heavy with anticipation, anxious
for the bookie's call.

I am from the nasal siren
of Fred Capossela's
"It is now post time"
that blared from the flicker
of the black and white portable
with the vertical hold
that never held
when the horses
hit the finish line.

I am from grocery money
hinged on whatever wizardry
remained in Whitey Ford's
failing left elbow

and the storm that erupted
when its magic
could no longer
beat the odds.

About the Author

Tony Gruenewald is the author of the collection *The Secret History of New Jersey*. His poems have been published in print and online publications and anthologies. He currently works as an archivist for major media organizations and has worked in advertising, broadcast journalism, and audio book production.

For more poetry by Tony visit

tonygruenewald.com

www.ingramcontent.com/pod-product-compliance
Lightning Source LLC
Chambersburg PA
CBHW031152090426
42738CB00008B/1297